Escape from Uncle Sam's
Plantation

Ed Temple

ISBN 978-1-64458-176-6 (paperback)
ISBN 978-1-64458-855-0 (hardcover)
ISBN 978-1-64458-177-3 (digital)

Christian Faith Publishing, Inc.
832 Park Avenue
Meadville, PA 16335
www.christianfaithpublishing.com

Printed in the United States of America

Introduction

I understand public schools are valued by some as necessary to prepare individuals to function in a civil society, but after teaching in the inner-city public schools for nearly two decades, I have concluded that public schools, especially inner-city public schools, are overall counterproductive. Thus, school-choice vouchers are necessary for many to escape Uncle Sam's plantation's deeply flawed system.

I believe our current public education system serves the interests of an ideology and squashes critical thinking and opposition to the ideology. It's becoming more and more apparent that schools, in particular government schools, are becoming part of a larger system of progressive ideology and indoctrination.

Teaching in Uncle Sam's plantation has brought me to the sad conclusions expressed in this book. The problems I will elaborate on are expressed by countless colleagues I have met across the country.

Parents and students would be best served with choice with regard to which environment best serves their needs. Parents should not be forced to pay twice for their child's education by sending them to a private school. Instead, each parent should be able to use whatever money is agreed upon as the per child expense in that particular state and use this money to pay for the school of their choice. Those that wanted to stay in public schools could do so while others could opt for the school that best fits them.

I realize the unions don't like vouchers because in a scenario of parents having choice, the virtual monopoly of Uncle Sam's schools would not be in the best financial interest of teachers or power of the unions. In the short-term plantation, (public) schools would lose students, and teachers would have to get new jobs that might not have the impressive salaries and benefits. Their fear of the public school system being damaged is little to do with the well-being of the students but almost entirely about the adults involved losing financially or unions losing their power and influence.

Clearly, public schools have been failing for many years. But they're doing more than that; they are teaching values that many parents do not agree with. Schools are becoming propaganda warehouses; and the student serve, being taught to take tests but not very often being taught all the sides of an issue or how to analyze information. Thus, the title for the government schools that sustains itself to society's detriment is aptly called Uncle Sam's plantation.

There are think tanks on each side of the issue about school-choice vouchers that make their case for and against vouchers. The debate for education choice leads to deeper discussions on the motivations of and the consequences of giving parents more options for their children.

The fact is that Uncle Sam's plantation (that I have had two decades to be entrenched) is no longer a place of learning to think but being taught what to think. The plantation cannot fix itself. The solution to ending Uncle Sam's monopoly is found in the last chapter of this book.

Chapter 1
The Plantation's Failed Attempts to Fix Problems It Helps Create

I was on the freeway in bumper-to-bumper traffic and noticed a police car driving next to me. He was driving while filling out paperwork. And it hit me. This is one of the problems with the climate in education today, just like it is in many fields that have so many regulations that it's hard to keep up with. There is way too much waste of time being bogged down with new legislation and paperwork as a result. This creates inefficiency, where educators spend way too much time being bogged down with compliance, creating less time to spend on preparedness for their students.

I enjoy asking colleagues who are proponents of testing if there is any evidence that the standardized testing for graduation has made students more effective students or proven beneficial in any way. Not one time have the proponents been able to say more than the standard line that can be paraphrased, "It helps legitimize the diploma."

Columbia University lists the pros and cons of standardized testing. The pros basically highlight having teachers focused across the country on particular objectives and being able to use unbiased data to access the performance of individual students compared to the districts in the area or even nationally; accountability is the biggest argument.

Columbia lists the cons, that, to me, far outweigh the benefits of standardized testing. The cons are extremely prevalent and dangerous to education. Cons, according to Columbia, include: Some students are just poor test takers. Testing causes teachers to teach to the test and adds more unhealthy stress to students and teachers. The final listed con is the unintended consequences of preparing for standardized testing includes often cutting recess and needed electives for more time to teach for the test (Columbia University, 2013).

For nearly two decades, I observed and was forced to participate in a climate of teaching to the test and observing the elective courses and teacher creativity fall by the wayside. Students will be required by most college and universities to take a readiness test before they will be admitted. The insatiable appetite of lawmakers to solve problems by taking up countless hours for testing and preparing for the testing is taking the fun out of learning for many teachers and students alike. Data from testing can be misleading and lead to school districts cheating students out of a quality education and more often than known, cheating to fudge the numbers.

The current education mandate is Every Student Succeeds Act signed by President Obama in 2015. ESSA is the newest plantation mandate although it is more flexible than the No Child Left Behind, but it still has the federal government holding states hostage. ESSA requires states to set achievement targets for students in schools. States must also set ambitious goals for groups of students who are the furthest behind, like students in special education. These goals should help close the gap with other students.

There are no federal penalties for struggling schools. Instead, these schools will get more funding and will have to develop a plan to improve. According to Emma Brown, "ESSA restores what they say was the intent of the original 1965 law: poor kids should get the extra help they need, regardless of where they go to school. This is huge news because the law says that school districts have to equitably share certain services with private schools, including, most prominently, Title I services for children from poor families" (Understood, 2018).

While I take no issue with helping poor kids, I believe the focus of education should be opportunities for all, not just one particular group. It seems in America, the middle class seems to get the least amount of attention even though it comprises of the vast majority of the country. Playing favorites or trying to redistribute resources is Marxism at its root.

It is safe to say ESSA will stir up the unions for sure and ultimately end up in courts all over the country. ESSA enacted means private schools that accept education voucher students will have more resources to improve student learning, be given desperately needed funds to survive, and have more competitive salaries. Currently, the median salary of private school teachers is 27 percent less than public schools, even less for Christian schools (Digest, 2009). I know this salary differential with my new Christian-school colleagues is very unsettling, to say the least. Our student body is similar in demographics and the staff works just as diligently as the public school teachers earning twice the salary and far more in monetary benefits.

Although the new ESSA being enforced by Betsy DeVos and the Department of Education gives parents and states back some authority from the last federal program No Child Left Behind, it's still the federal government intruding on education. It also continues the process of rewarding failing schools by allowing them to get more money to fix problems the day created. In a sense, they are incentivizing failing. To make it worse, a failing school in California has to be propped up a tax money from Ohio.

In one school I taught at for eighteen years, nearly every attempt to fix a problem resulted in a new set of problems. Of course, to fix a problem, the plantation gets countless federal, state, local, and community funds to support the system. The district disproportionately sent resources, including extra teachers and a new $34 million refurbished building in hopes to "restore the roar." The school remained and remains on the news almost weekly with negative reports of events occurring during school so outlandish that the news caught wind.

For ten consecutive years, the teachers at the school I taught recognized the huge distraction the clothing worn was becoming for students who wanted school to be a place to learn. Parents were sent a mail, or if they showed up, given the right to vote for uniforms or to keep the status quo. A non-vote kept the status quo. Not one of the ten years did the parents did not send the paper with their vote in. So finally, the administration, figuring the parents would not vote either way, changed the format of the vote to say there would be a school uniform unless the parents vote no. So the uniform policy was adopted.

The policy was a huge success at first. The kids looked great, and the community financed or donated the clothes for those who could not afford the polo shirt and khaki pants. The school atmosphere was the best ever! Kids were learning and staying out of trouble until a few challenged the policy by complaining to the district officials. After just a few complaints, the district told the administration that the policy cannot be enforced. No reason was given. Keep in mind the uniforms at the school were for free to any student who could not afford to purchase one. Countless time was spent getting a system in place to get the uniform policy and putting all the what-ifs in place.

The district's lack of support or backbone to this failing school was and still is killing the chances for success for this school. To be sure, the district rarely backs up any of its schools. The results were teachers dealing with more discipline and teaching less and students who felt rules were only to be followed until adults gave in to the students wishes.

I had worked for three superintendents, and not much ever changed. The turnover rate for teachers, administrators, and students in every school in my district and most large inner-city school districts is devastating to learning.

My former employment in the state's largest district is not unique in its loss of moral high ground. Morality in leadership and within schools has steadily reflected society's decline and has done more to encourage the downtrend than to stop the bleeding.

Why have morals declined in schools?

On June 25, 1962, the United States Supreme Court effectively ended school prayer (Engel v. Vitale), and in 1963, in Abington School District v. Schempp, the court decided against Bible readings in public schools. Clearly, there is plenty of evidence of the damage these court cases led to.

According to one California State College professor, since 1963, there have been five negative developments in the nation's public schools:

- Academic achievement has plummeted including SAT scores.
- Increased rate of out-of-wedlock births
- Increase in illegal drug use
- Increase in juvenile crime
- Deterioration of school behavior (Redmen, 2018)

The government schools cannot fix the problem because they are the problem. First off, the federal government has no constitutional right to be involved with state schools. But all forms of government should find ways of not allowing innovation getting in the way. In a society that prides itself respecting and yearning for diversity, education diversity should not be an exception. Parents should decide what is best for "Little Johnny," not "Uncle Sam."

Spending money is not the answer either. Otherwise, America would lead the world in international benchmarks. In fact, besides Norway and Switzerland, the US spends more than every other country in the world (Pflaum, 2018). As Americans, we should realize the foundational concepts that have given us the exceptional standard of living. The government virtual monopoly is clearly failing.

For this book, Uncle Sam's plantation is defined as the inner-city public school system, but at times, this also includes public schools in general. The government schools cannot seem to get out of their own way.

In my experience, before change in policy or program for the better is fully implemented, the system gives up and starts another program. Inevitably, over time, teachers realize this trial and quit method of operation and lose their motivation to implement. Of course, the result of the endless new programs that are not given a chance to work are schools loaded with unmotivated staff.

Systematically, students are failed by how discipline is or isn't dealt with. I will go further into details on this topic, but let me illustrate an example: in a meeting deciding who would be allowed to attend this trip, there was general agreement on a handful of kids that should not be taken because of their history of misbehavior during a normal day in class. I was lucky in successfully surprising this teacher-leadership group into taking these students with the caveat that the students would have to sit next to me on the bus and stay with me during the trip. They reluctantly agreed after I shocked them with explaining to the group how these disruptive students were who most needed to attend trips like this one, that part of the problem with their behavior problems, ostensibly, is their lack of motivation to learn or just simply being academically behind. After all, the most common strategy to deal with behavior problems is (as most administrators will routinely audibly threaten) "ten days," meaning, students get up to ten days of out-of-school detention.

The bottom line is that Uncle Sam's plantation is failing students in many ways. Overall, the plantation system attempts to solve problems that exacerbate the current problem or creates new problems to deal with. The system is broken but clearly is not able to fix itself.

Chapter 2
Why Does the Plantation Lower the Bar?

Glenn Beck said it best, "States, now forced to compete for federal dollars by hitting certain National benchmarks, are in set of eyes to lie, cheat, and steal to get the results they need" (Conform, Beck).

Our district, like many other in Uncle Sam's plantation, has been found guilty of changing grades and attendance records systematically. Schools get funding based on school attendance and earn their reputation based on graduation rates.

If you are a teacher that wants to be left alone (fly under the radar), just make sure students are passing, and that the students who normally get on the honor roll maintain a *B* or higher. As soon as you break these unwritten but highly understood rules, watch out!

Span across the country to see the countless grading and attendance scams that have been made public. The unintended consequences of attaching funding or financial incentives to attendance and matriculation is bending the rules, cheating, and when all is said, lowering the standards and watering down the education.

In D.C. schools, one teacher responded about the pressure they felt describing, "When I informed people of the amount of students that were failing my class, it was kind of conveyed to me that that number was very high, and I should make it lower" (McGee). Not too far from D.C., similar pressure was evident in New York. One assistant principal e-mailed teachers guidance, in which she warned that 150 students were set to flunk classes, and that the school graduation rate loomed at less than 50 percent, emphasizing, "Our benchmark of a 60 percent graduation rate is nonnegotiable" (Edelman).

The pressure to pass comes at Uncle Sam even at the college and university level. The University of Polytech staff are under increasing pressure to pass more students to meet government targets, a survey has found (Redmond, *Pressure to Pass*).

My personal reputation as a teacher by most of my students was that I was the teacher that supposedly gave the most work and was their hardest teacher to pass. I was shocked at this assessment by students at first, given the fact that I gave homework that should take thirty minutes and made reasonable tests that students were told exactly what to expect on the test. The handful of students that were focused, bothered to take notes, and studied their notes for a few minutes were generally getting no less than a B.

What I found out in teacher meetings was that most teachers had given up on assigning homework. Oftentimes homework was only a small fraction of the grade, so students could skip doing it and still easily pass. Teachers were passing students that missed more than the allowed days to miss before failing.

The district I taught in, the largest in the state, lowered the requirements for letter grades so that more could pass. A 1.0 used to be a passing D, but now with a D- passing, they're only requiring a .5. What a joke!

Routinely, individually, or as a staff, teachers were told to find ways to get students to pass. And of course, there is more documentation and ways to get a poor evaluation for every kid that you fail. For years, teachers at my school would be amazed at how many students had their grades changed by administrators so students would be eligible to play sports. Of course, this is not ethical or legal.

The more lenient you grade means more committees you get placed on to run, the better opportunities you get to advance in much higher-paying and more prestigious jobs within the district or in a better situation. In other words, pass the kids along and get a promotion. Failing students will get you a poor evaluation, lead to not getting your contract renewed, getting fired, or pressured to resign. Generally, in my former district, and I can safely assume many if not most large districts across America, administrators are mostly former teachers that passed the most students along are the ones that have bad reputation as teachers. Unfortunately, these same administrators will become the evaluators for the teachers in their buildings.

Students realize how to play the game and get their parents to understand the game that they don't need to do homework or work very hard, and the teachers will eventually be pressured to cave in and pass them. Unfortunately, the parents often do not understand the damage these unwritten rules do to their children. But the parents are only playing by the unwritten rules, so it is hard to blame them.

Academics are not the only form of lowering the standards the plantation system live by. Disciplining students is tricky too. Administrators will be quick to overturn a teacher's attempt at curbing problems.

Our school had a problem with students being tardy to class. We were told to lock our doors when the bell rings. Not long after locking the doors, we must take electronic attendance while settling students down that often were very wound up talking about the fight that just occurred or that was going to occur after school. Meanwhile, countless students were knocking on the door in increments over the next fifteen minutes. And in a half an hour or so, an administrator would find a student cutting class and let the student themselves.

In order to curb the tardy situation, I would make students wait in the hall until after I took attendance. This drastically reduced interruptions and led the kids losing their authority over the situation. The consequence of the wait time was immediate. Students stopped coming late. Interruptions were minimized, and the students were documented as tardy.

The administration believed this was cruel. They even announced on the PA system for all to hear, "Teachers, please leave your rooms unlocked and let students into your classroom." Soon, students were back at coming late unless on rare occasions a "hall sweep" was announced.

Students are given a handbook in the district that states that nine unexcused tardies per grading period results in a failing grade regardless of the current grade in the class.

The average student at the school I taught in was absent fifteen days per quarter and tardy to school about 50 percent of the time. So many students were late that two teachers would have to help the attendance secretary sign students in every period of the school day.

A teacher like myself would be brave enough to enforce the district policy of nine unexcused days as a failing grade. Instead of allowing the student to fail, the school would tell the parent how to get around the issue. The secretary or administrator would print out the dates absent and have the parent write a note for each date explaining how the student was sick. Just about any excuse was accepted to avoid being labeled "unexcused."

In the school's defense, every trick in the book was attempted to fix the attendance problem. Students were given monopoly money to be used to buy cool things on Fridays. Students were suspended if caught in hall sweeps. Lunch detentions were tried. Nothing worked. The culture of disrespect was embedded into the system from day one.

Uncle Sam's students start disrespecting authority when they come to school wearing clothes showing their underwear knowing the rules against it. So many teachers and administrators give up trying to enforce this rule because of the heavy resistance to it, like being called a racist for enforcing the rule. It takes about a week or so before they realize coming to class or school on time is not important.

Plantation teachers regularly talk about how easy they make the tests to ensure more students pass. Teachers often go over actual question or even pass out the actual test, including final exams, for students to study to pass. The vast majority of students still fail, but they quickly realize a curve is coming.

Chapter 3
The Plantation's Unholy Alliances

Teaching in Uncle Sam's plantation is easy to see the flaws in the system. Teachers that go against the system are quickly put back in their place. The administrators and teachers must "toe the line" or face unfavorable consequences. And who is the powerful coercive force?

Dr. Steve Perry, author of *Push Has Come to Shove*, puts the unions into their proper place, "The teachers' union leadership for the past generation has actively fought every form of educational reform." In other words, the union is part of the plantation system. There's an unhealthy relationship between the union and the Democratic Party. Over the last twenty years, nearly every candidate that they endorse is the Democrat. When teachers' union, National Education Association (NEA), has big meetings, they invite only speakers from the Democratic Party.

During elections, teachers are not allowed to, but they go ahead and wear their pins and shirts expressing their candidate choice. As long as it's a Democrat, nothing will be said to you. But even alleged support of a candidate that is not a Democrat, in reaction, is swift.

And of course, the union fights against school-choice vouchers, and consequently, the democratic leadership will not allow any dissension from their members on this issue. State Teacher Retirement System (STRS) is horribly underfunded across the country largely because of the politicians giving in to the desires of the teachers' unions, giving benefits much more lucrative than the private market.

It is not just the unions that make the system flawed. If you are teaching about religion, even if it's part of the curriculum, as soon as the Bible is discussed or alluded to, inevitably, a student or parent complains, and the teacher ends up in trouble.

The vast majority of teachers align themselves with the Democrat Party, and some of these teachers alienate anyone not falling in line with the Democratic Party as "racists" or a vast array of many other names or just pressure those that do not follow along.

About the only time unions are cooperative with the school administration is to help get rid of the conservative teachers. Before a hearing is ever made, before the due process can take its course, the union leaders within the school talk to the union leaders that represent teachers in hearings. The union leaders at the hearings make deals with the school administrators that give more severe consequences and little defense for conservative teachers.

Parents might be shocked if they were to find out whom all the guest speakers that are brought in for teachers' training. They might be justifiably upset if they knew what all this training was about. But the teachers' union and the board of education have their far-left agenda to promote. I realize that not all boards of education are far left, but the teachers' unions, except for a few Christian unions that represent a very small number of teachers, are extremely far left in their views.

Teachers are trained throughout the year that African American students cannot be taught like the other students. They are also told they should be communicating in Ebonics in order to relate to the students.

I never forget one time we had a guest speaker by the name of Dr. Winbush. Winbush played video clips from the movie called *Crash*. I wasn't sure what the point of the video clips was but maybe to make us all feel uncomfortable. It was abundantly clear by the end of the grueling session, the white teachers were supposed to accept the fact that cops, teachers or whomever else are white are systematically racists, and that we must accept that fact. I made sure I went back and had some e-mail conversations going back and forth with Dr. Winbush. I concluded I was correct in assuming that he had some real problems with white people. I came to find out he wrote a book about how America should pay reparations and was even on *The Oprah Winfrey Show*.

There were other trainings that suggested teachers teach about the sexuality of major figures in history books, especially if they might have had homosexual secret lifestyles. We were told that students have the right to know about which of the presidents and other founding fathers were possibly gay.

Teachers aren't the only ones being overwhelmed with the agenda of the far left. Students could count on annual presentations from planned parenthood and could expect to get condoms regularly handed out as well. One counselor would tell kids that they should express their homosexual feelings by attending queer dances. Another homosexual teacher would post the gay-straight alliance meetings. We had had at least five students that were identified as heterosexuals that after a few sessions with the gay-straight alliance, became committed homosexuals. There are a disproportionate number of homosexuals in union leadership, as well as at every school in the district-leading schools or educators.

Our district happened to have a homosexual superintendent that just retired in 2018. All over the school district office buildings and in the secondary schools, you could find pamphlets advertising gay parades and other homosexual activities for students and faculty, including to attend queer day dances. One school in the city announced regular commitment times to attending the gay parade or other gay activities around the city and sent groups regularly to attend these events. I am sure it was a coincidence (wink wink) that teachers were told the word that will trigger a consequence over *any* other is "gay." If a kid said, "That's gay," this is intolerable and would lead to immediate and severe consequences. Keep in mind, students cursing out students was normal in the district and often went without a consequence. But any statement with the word "gay" trumped all other that if said, garnered a punishment.

Every year there's an increasing number of training, the so-called training that focused on telling teachers how inherently racist schools are and how white teachers are inherently racists. Never mind the fact that over 75 percent of the teachers they are telling us are white themselves. It's no wonder the morale is down on all the surveys year-in and year-out when the majority of your teachers are white and are singled out as though they are predestined to be the problem.

Chapter 4
Exposing the Daily Life in Plantation Schools

If people only knew what went on public schools, they would definitely rethink sending their children to the public schools. Whether it is the controversial speakers, representatives from planned parenthood passing out condoms, the teaching of sex education for elementary students, and many other daily events students get exposed to or indoctrinated in. Parents are not considered when most decisions are made by school leadership.

I've been teaching for over two decades and have seen just about everything. Of course, the situation in the school system has become worse and worse as the values have gone further and further to the left. Kids used to avoid bad language around teachers when I first started teaching, but today, students do not even worry about the consequence of using vulgar language around even the head principal. But they don't stop at bad language.

It is a regular occurrence that teachers are cussed at and threatened by students and by their parents. Oftentimes, after being threatened by a student, I would like most teachers kick the student out of class. But instead of disciplining the student, the administrator would just give the student a warning and send them right back to class. Of course, the student comes back into class and continues to make a scene.

In case you think that what I have gone through is rare, my wife also worked in the same building for years with me and has many of the same stories to tell. In the teacher workshops I have gone to in the last twenty years, the same stories come up in matters of which Uncle Sam's school teachers were from.

The girls' restrooms were haven for used condoms and underwear. Even though there were cameras everywhere in the buildings, the security would tell you how regular making out, including sexual behaviors, were done even in the hallway. At least a few times a year, kids were caught having sex in classrooms usually after school, and in some cases, even during school.

Bad language and sexual activity are not the only things going on in Uncle Sam's plantation. Bullying and fighting, especially gang-related fights, are the norm. You wouldn't believe how many girls get into fights on a daily basis. These fights are not just one or two slaps, they are not down drag out people, jumping, or kicking, and of course, sometimes using weapons. A great percentage of the kids are forced to join some type of gang even in the preteen years. Gang graffiti is everywhere.

Fighting and classroom disturbances are so common that when the teacher calls down for help, they might be lucky to get somebody come up, and if they do come up to help, it will be regularly a half an hour later. If there's not a fight going on in the room, students are talking about a fight that just happened or that is going to happen. Very little time is focused on actually in the morning, whatever the curriculum has in store. Every ounce of instruction is a struggle. Many kids look forward to daily doses of drama.

Countless times I asked students why they came back to our school after leaving for another school. The two most popular responses were that the other school was too strict and that one or the other school was too boring compared to the daily drama that our school had. Each opportunity where teachers from other schools in the district were trained together, venting of similar stories was the norm. Consequently, training for teachers became venting for teachers about similar experiences as mentioned.

At times, the media finds out about things that happen, but believe me, there is so much more that goes on. Teachers will be fired if they ever report it. The media is not allowed to report on it (I should know. I offered a reporter to come in as a guest to witness it).

It is a regular occurrence to find illegal drugs, guns, knives, and other dangerous items in lockers or in book bags. One time, a boy pulled out a gun and a knife on another student in the same day, and this was never even talked about at school, and of course, never made it to the news.

I decided to ask one of my students attending the Christian school that I taught at how she ended up at our school. She explained how she was going to a public school in Columbus that I am very aware is like most in district (Ohio's largest school system)—a failing school. This student is still not the most ambitious student, but she escaped involvement in fighting almost daily at her former public school. She said that being picked on necessitated fighting to get respect, or more bullying toward her would continue on worse terms. The student pointed out how our school has similar demographics to where we both are now, but the Christian school has a far better atmosphere and quality of education. She has gone to our school for over four years without coming close to getting into a fight.

Plantation schools are like prison: nobody wants to talk about what goes on in them. To the outside world, you probably won't understand unless you're actually seeing it for yourself. Just in the past several years, I've had two students that murdered two other students that I had in class. One of my students was a founder of a gang that nearly all of the local gangs were splinter groups from the original gang. Nearly every boy and girl attending the school was (and likely still are) affiliated with a gang.

Students at my plantation school were given bus transportation during the school day to attend the funeral for the gang leader of the largest teen gang in the city. It was even allowed for students to hang poster boards all over the wall of this student as well as other students in his gang, throwing up gang signs, and holding guns. He was only in the eighth grade when he was killed not far from the school. As a middle schooler, he took over a gang his family was running. He was and is, posthumously, a huge influence not only at our school but all around the city.

The teachers are forced to be part of the plantation system. It doesn't take long to find out that only progressives are free to be boisterous, biased, and the most radical are from the progressive or the left perspective. These teachers can regularly say, "The white man" in a conspiratorial way that often leads many students to be angry toward the white students and faculty. I would often hear about or listen in the halls all the antiwhite propaganda that was never questioned by the leadership in the school. Of course, these teachers were promoted quickly.[1]

Other teachers teach the *theory* of evolution as if it is a fact, without a hint of criticism. Other controversial issues like global warming (once called cooling), now morphed to climate change, and now climate fluctuations, and in general the left perspective, are taught to be unquestionable fact.

An example of the plantation mentality was when I had a mock trial that was in my curriculum, the Scopes Trial.

[1] http://abc11.com/education/raleigh-parent-upset-about-white-privilege-paper-sent-home-with-student/3297299/

Two atheist (now Christian) students told their mother that students were making fun of them, and that they felt uncomfortable about their atheist beliefs because of the emotion in the trial. I was called immediately and put in a conference with the principal, the parent, and the daughters to discuss why I decided to teach what was in the curriculum!

On another occasion, I was teaching a concept by having the kids debate. Four different classes had three different outcomes. Students were also part of the debate scoring of each other. The topic was the various main religions, proving which is the best. This apparently was too controversial to one teacher who believed I was teaching students to hate Judaism (she was Jewish). I told her the truth, that in one class, the students debating for the Judaism won, which seemed to settle her down a little. But it did not underscore the point. Students in the plantation are not supposed to think for themselves, but just repeat what they are told.

During a conversation with a progressive history teacher, I asked her if she would be interested in showing her class a video by Dinesh D'Souza. Her reply was that she would never show the video because she disagreed with it. When pressed on what she disagreed with, she gave an incoherent answer. I continued to press the issue and asked her if students should be shown a perspective she disagreed with. I asked her if she knew D'Souza was a professor and a historian. I also told her that I was like her, a licensed social studies teacher that agreed with and could find no flaw with this video. She ended the discussion because she had no interest in showing this video because it did not represent her point of view. Just the students are taught not to, she could not attempt to open her eyes to the other perspective. Keep in mind the progressives always rant about fairness and equality, being open-minded.

Plantation schools are led and taught mostly by teachers who have the mind-set of the anti-D'Souza, really anti-conservative. Daily ranting about Republicans, especially if there is a Republican running for president or that is currently the president. The ranting is the same tired comments about how (no matter who that Republican is) this person is racist, hates the poor, wants to take away welfare, is a heartless Nazi, etc. There is no filter or balance when it comes to politics. Teachers no better than to give balance since this leads to discipline in one form or another.

The bias does not stop with politics; it takes form in every subject. Science class promotes just about any religion or cause unless it hints at creation or any criticism of the current theory being promoted from the progressive agenda. Evolution is not taught as a flawed theory made popular by a nonscientist but taught as a fact that disproves the creation story.

The plantation indoctrination does not stop with science. Students are encouraged to attend or join queer dances, gay groups, (gay) pride parades, and more. Required reading would not make many parents very happy if they knew some of the sultry material being read.

Once, I inadvertently veered from the plantation's unwritten rules. I allowed students to read an excerpt from a book that I did not realize had a Bible verse on the bottom of paper containing the excerpt. The verse was neither read nor did I even realize it was there until after I was called to the principal's office to explain why I violated the unwritten rules. I found out fifteen years later that this was in my file!

The Scopes Trial is part of the curriculum and very important to study in order to understand American history. Apparently this was too offensive because I was once again called to meet with the parent, her twins that were both my students, and the atheist administrator (later fired for unrelated reasons). I quickly resolved the issue after explaining the emotion from the twins was from the mock trial and not the topic, and that the topic was and still is part of the curriculum!

Chapter 5
The Darwin Effect on Uncle Sam's Plantation

The founder of the Creation Museum and a world renowned Christian scientist, Ken Ham, explains the seeds of racism were planted soon after Darwin's version of evolution became widespread, stating, "This theory [Darwin's theory] logically implies that certain races are more ape-like than they might be human." Ham went on to say,

> The widely held view was that blacks evolved from the strong but less intelligent gorillas.
>
> Within decades evolution was used to justify whites turning on themselves and who could forget the Nazi conception of racial superiority. But Darwin's theory didn't stop warping minds there … Darwinian superiority complexes went and still go from sea to sea. Serbs felt superiority with Croats, Australia and the Aborigines, North America with the so-called savage Native Americans, Japanese towards Europeans, Europeans towards Japanese, and not stopping with the Ku Klux Klan. Today there is a Christian identity movement that believes Jews and blacks are not even human! (Ham)

Darwinian evolution is taught in Uncle Sam's plantation all over the country. Evolution is taught as if it were a fact even though it's not even qualified as a theory since macroevolution is not observable or testable.

My favorite remark to the creation skeptics is from apologist Frank Turek, author of *I Don't Have Enough Faith to be an Atheist*, often says that clearly, many of the atheists rely on Darwin's theory to prove their case. The progressive media had talking heads attack Billy Nye after (based on media reactions) Ken Ham won the debate in *Bill Nye the Science Guy*. Ham supporters might have seen this as proving that when put to the test, evolution falls apart.

The Scopes Trial temporarily put references to Darwin on hold or made them less obvious. Some biology textbooks even began to include religious quotations. Groups such as the California State board of education argued that these quotations made biology textbooks worthy of adoption because the quotations showed that the books were "tactfully written" and presented evolution as a "theory and not as an established fact" (Moore). California was even on board to give respect to the Bible!

Fast forward a few or court cases and the Bible is playing second fiddle to having faith in a dangerous racist propagator. Consequently, we go from a Bible view that all were purposefully created in God's image to the view that humans are just a random evolutionary action that has tiers of one group being more supposedly more advanced than another. Inevitably, pitting groups against each other.

Darwinist education had a major role in the formation of communist leaders like Pol Pot, Hitler, Stalin, Mao, and many others whose leadership based on evolution led to one hundred million deaths. The Russian dictator Joseph Stalin was religious in his youth but became an atheist in large part because of Darwin's books. Mao, communist dictator in China, killed millions of people, stated that "Chinese socialism is founded upon Darwin and the theory of evolution." The religion of evolution has unparalleled deadly collateral damage (*Communism and Natural Selection*).

The plantation system is not neutral. It is anti-Christian, anti-reason. There is no room for dissent.

> A federal judge Thursday ordered a suburban Atlanta school system to remove stickers from its high school biology textbooks that call evolution "a theory, not a fact," saying the disclaimers are an unconstitutional endorsement of religion." The judge feels questioning evolution is the same as endorsing religion? After all, the judge might not want to know calling

"The Theory of Evolution," a theory is like calling the "Honorable judge" honorable. Calling Evolution a theory is a far stretch since theories must be "observable and testable," which neither can be done in the case of macroevolution. Often times judicial activist judges, whom ignore first amendment rights, are the plantation crackers. When a school gets the notion to be "free" the crackers whip them back into line. (NBC News)

Uncle Sam's plantation schools are fulfilling what Orwell describes in 1984, "Who controls the past controls the future. Who controls the present controls the past. War is peace. Freedom is slavery. Ignorance is strength." Because I have intermittently taught social studies and math courses (because of my dual certification), I realize that Howard Zinn's portrayal of history is, without a doubt, the most prevalent. I am ashamed to admit that even I allowed myself to teach from books that promoted this version. It took me several years to do my own research outside of the university curriculum and high school curriculum to discover the truth and understanding that totally changes the outlook on how I understand history.

Sadly, Howard Zinn's *A People's History of the United States* has been used throughout many schools as part of their curriculum and deemed as historically accurate but is at best revisionist history, according to Dinesh D'Souza (Breitbart).

The year *America: Imagine the World Without Her*, the documentary film came out and was the top grossing documentary of 2016 and his book was also a *New York Times* best seller for fifteen weeks (The Hollywood Reporter). As a teacher of history, I can say his documentary and book take a refreshing but honest and accurate depiction of American history. I personally find it hard to argue against his presentation of facts or his analysis thereof.

The National Association of Scholars (NAS) reported:

> Although the Obama administration replaced national civics and U.S. history exams with technology assessments in 2013, their results were consistently poor: In 2010, the last time the history test was administered, students performed worse on it than on any other NAEP test. Less than half the

eighth-graders knew the purpose of the
Bill of Rights, and only 1 in 10 could
pick a definition of the system of checks
and balance. (The Federalist)

For the past few years, there have been seemingly
Orwellian efforts to take down "offensive statues" that contribute to understanding our history. But in the last two decades,
working with progressives, some of which worked for political
candidates on both sides of the aisle, I learned there is very
little difference between a progressive and a communist with
respect to government responsibilities and power.

The Communist Manifesto aims at destroying the
national identity and replacing it with a global identity
as does the progressive education taught in the plantation system. The manifesto also portrays Christianity
as an outdated problem that has already been cancelled
out by rational thought, just as progressives try to teach
with Darwinism and secular humanism. Marxists and
progressives also believe Christianity is intertwined with
free-market capitalism. To the progressive and Marxist, a
strong centralized government is the solution. Of course,
this is in dire contrast with America's historically free
market and freedom of expression method of operation.

Based on the fact that the teacher unions are progressive and that most teachers identify with progressive ideology, it is no wonder these unions scream so loud when any money is diverted to Christian schools. After all, Christianity is a threat to their secular humanistic belief system, so many of these union members have been indoctrinating to captive young minds for years in schools, in the mainstream media, and now in the mind-controlling social media from phones, which kids and adults alike can't seem to put down.

Although far less a red state than in the past, Texas is trying to do something about the progressive secular onslaught. "The board is to vote on a sweeping purge of alleged liberal bias in Texas school textbooks in favor of what attorney Cynthia Dunbar says really matters: a belief in America as a nation chosen by God as a beacon to the world, and free enterprise as the cornerstone of liberty and democracy" (McGreal).

Donald Trump used statements like Dunbar's refreshing American words of exceptionalism throughout his campaign and continues to since he has been president. It is encouraging that he speaks this way of his country because I'm sure many are like myself, feeling this needs to be said. Americans don't appreciate enough of how blessed we are. Sometimes when you're in the eye of the storm, you don't recognize there is a storm.

Teaching in the plantation system for almost two decades was enough proof to show me how depressing Darwinism as a pervasive thought is. My current Christian school employment is a far contrast to this. I have heard a few students at my school say they don't believe our school is very Christian. I quickly respond to this statement when I hear it. My basic response is the mere fact that we can evaluate our relationship with God is not allowed in the plantation schools. The students in the public schools were shamed into not wanting to associate with calling themselves Christian.

When I press the students for a reason why they don't believe their school is a Christian school, they inevitably say because so many kids do not behave like Christians should. Interestingly enough, it is usually the pot calling the kettle black. When I point out the obvious distinctions in the school like going to chapel on Fridays, having Bible class, praying for each other, and all teachers infusing Bible instruction into their lessons, the students quickly see the error in their thoughts.

There were only a couple of minor scuffles in my current school this year. When the scuffle was over, the conversation about the scuffle was over. In the plantation schools, it is common to have several fights every day that often involve gangs and some type of continued violence throughout the school year. The conversations in class in the plantation school system revolve around fighting. At my school, the consistent conversation is about competing to get into something athletic or academic. Kids here care about one another and do not mind showing it.

Government schools have agendas that Christian schools teach about but left open to debate. Government schools want students to believe in whatever the latest scientific fad is and believe in a world that is explained without intelligent design. Many scientists are admitting the possibility of God's existence, but government students rarely learn outside the progressive ideological box.

Chapter 6
Government Meddling

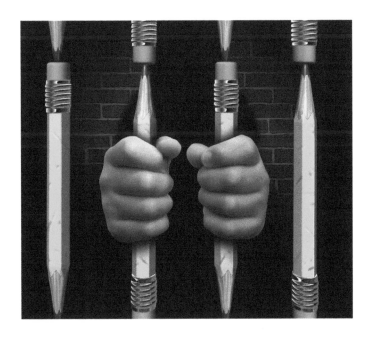

Whether it is No Child Left Behind or whatever the flavor of the day is, the big government solution just adds to the school budget woes and ensuing chaos. Schools might need support but not puppet masters.

With the Obama administration suing and pressuring districts to cut their suspension rates, it became racist to suspend African American students. Although the number of suspensions and discipline documented went down, the behavior and violence actually went up in districts that complied with the Obama administration. One teacher in Oklahoma was quoted as saying, "We were told referrals would not require suspensions unless there was blood."

As a result of students knowing they're not getting suspended, in Oklahoma City public schools, cursing, hitting, and screaming at teachers all increased because teachers were told to ignore these behaviors.

But bad behavior didn't stop with words. In Saint Paul, Minnesota, teachers were told to only report the worst offenses. And although reports of violence declined, the violence actually increased. Saint Paul teachers also were taught by the district-sponsored Pacific Education Group (PEG) that white privilege was the cause of the disproportionate suspensions for African American students. PEG pressured 180 districts to drastically reduce suspension rates.

The result of PEG in Saint Paul schools was teachers being questioned of trying to discipline African American students. Of course, the district wanted to know if the teacher was being a racist when disciplining a student.

Consequently in 2014–2015, assaults against teachers doubled and many disrespectful behaviors also increased (*The Corrupt Classroom*).

Of course, one of the unintended but predictable consequences of keeping troubled children in classrooms instead of suspending them is the negative impact on other students, as well as scores.

Teachers are pressured to pass students. If you don't pass enough students, believe me, your job will be in jeopardy. The district I taught in was still manipulating grades and attendance even after the district was indicted in a huge grading scam and attendance scam. The pressure from the district officials was put on administrators and administrators to teachers that involved coercing or just changing lose grades from failing to passing.

The quickest way to lose your teaching job is to have a high failure rate. There are endless meetings for teachers to find ways to pass kids. The basic premise is the high failure rate because of everything and everyone, except the student.

Every year a different program is tried (and most often fails) to address student engagement and attempt to lower the failure rate. Oftentimes the programs are extremely costly. Teachers are put into endless trainings where they are lectured, and while being lectured, the teachers are told not to lecture!

Teachers are effectively being told that the failure rate is because of the teachers' failure to engage students. White teachers are told they need to step out of their "privilege" and teach the minority of the students differently.

At the school I was teaching for nearly two decades, the average student missed fifteen days per quarter. When they did come to school, about one-third were tardy. The district policy stated nine unexcused absences results in failure. Apparently the rules were not supposed to be enforced at my school because one way or another, students are seldom held accountable. And teachers who have high failure rates tread so very lightly knowing they will be called to the carpet.

Ron Clark points out in his book *Move Your Bus* how difficult it is to fire tenured teachers that are ineffective or have done something unethical. Clark spends time citing examples and stressing how he hires the best but ignores what most schools find credible, in particular the teacher's resumé. While Mr. Clark is highly successful with hiring great teachers and has unbelievable results to back his approach, the government schools keep repeating the same tired and failed ways because of their being virtually above reproach and unaccountable.

One time I was on an interview to make a transfer within the district I was teaching in. Some of the questions let me know how trivial the hiring process can be. Unlike Ron Clark, who wants to ask questions that allow the personality and clues to what kind of teacher you are, the government school just asked the predictable questions and even worse. The question I emphatically disliked the most was pertaining to homework. One interviewer on the team asked me how I graded homework and whether it was important. In other words, it was a trap. If the panel was against giving homework, I would be doomed to say I believed it as important and doomed if I said I did not value homework if this group valued it. Both trains of thought are debated by teachers as ongoing issues.

Why complain about an interview question? A few years ago, my school system was trying to do script teaching by the minute. This failed. By they found an outside loophole—curriculum guides. In these guides, the game plan was laid out. Most teachers just followed these like robots. But how did this promote creativity?

Of course, the curriculum guide is set up to pass some standardized test. Consequently, the plantation schools are very good at "teaching to the test" but produce students while the schools are largely not maximizing the teacher efficacy nor the student's potential.

Why do the government schools pressure teachers to teach to tests? Look no further than local, state, and federal meddling. The Common Core State Standards Initiative is a perfect example of destroying schools and forcing schools to toe the line. Pushed by the Obama administration and Bill Gates, the Common Core has been a disaster from the start. It is not hard to find a parent or student not baffled by the nonsensical math technique being forced on teachers to teach students or the politically charged English literature class topics and recommended lessons.

I do not believe I ever met one teacher that was happy with Common Core. Parents who were medical doctors or engineers were complaining that helping their kids with their math was becoming impossible because of the illogical and tiresome unorthodox step required to complete assignments. To make matters worse, the assignments were often graded on the process, not the answer!

Literature teachers were not happy with the standards and suggest readings changing either. The Common Core veers away from the classics and instead, "informative texts."

I do not want to get into the specifics of the Common Core or any other government program but highlight the fact that government intrusion is often a hindrance to education. The politicians should consider balancing budgets more and spend less time trying to engineer and manipulate outcomes. Just think of how much money was wasted on the Common Core books and training teachers to teach the newest faux paus technique. Many school systems wised up to leaving out of the Common Core curriculum, but only after spending millions to start and maintain it. Now they will have to spend money reverting back or reinventing the wheel.

Chapter 7
Bias Against

Teachers and students in public schools will notice the bias from getting certified to teach to training while teaching. It doesn't take you long to do a Yahoo, Bing, or Google search to find a consistently shamed or humiliated for just being.

Whether it is a musical the high school was pressured to cancel because a white actor got the lead role or how a teacher explains to the students how white people are born racists, even though whites (these ideologies say) go to great lengths to hide their innate racism. Stories with examples of government schools displaying anti-white (especially male) bias are countless and daily. Teachers are given free books by administrators and are taught in "professional development," training several times a year how the teachers must learn to relate to students of color, and part of the problem getting students to learn is because of the unintended and subconscious racism white teachers have.

Bias against white students and teachers aren't the only groups singled out. Just being a male, especially a highly manly male. Christina Hoff Sommer, the author of *The War Against Boys*, wonders why faulty research that is not peer reviewed is driving education in teacher workshops and when educating children. Sommer goes on to mention how influential intellectuals in educations were in promoting the deconstruction of masculinity. I kid you not! Based on what is currently socially acceptable with respect to gender identities, it seems to make sense part of the reason why. This social engineering of what the intellectuals deem is the new masculinity (feminizing might be a better description) has been going on since 2000.

Girls are far more likely to be offered single-sex classrooms, but the beneficiary of single-sex classrooms are boys. Scores for single-sex boys classrooms improve 20 percent on average. Chancellor Rudy Crew established an all-girls public school in East Harlem that was such a great success that he was asked to start an all-boys school. Mr. Crew said he regarded the girls school as a form of reparation for past educational practices that neglected girls. But Sommers counters Chancellor Crew by pointing out that almost all the African American educational gains in higher education have been African American women (Sommer, *The War Against Boys*).

Kevin Carey, a Washington D.C. think tank author and vice president of Education Policy and Knowledge Management at New America, likes the idea vouchers. But not surprisingly, he takes exception with vouchers escaping the plantation. He points out that liberals want their kids in union schools and conservatives want their kids to go to Christian schools. So what's the problem? Carey unfortunately believes the Christian school option should be off the table. But why does Carey feel this way? Doesn't Carey believe that parents should have the right to choose a Christian school? The likely recipients of vouchers are either religious or nonunionized private schools; therefore, Carey, and it is safe to assume a great number of others from his perspective, do not believe parents should have the choice to leave the plantation unless it is to attend a different plantation school (Carey, *The Atlantic*).

President Trump has repeated the phrase (running for president and each speech during his first year as president), "In America, we don't worship government—we worship God." Yet in public schools and now at most sporting events, prayer is replaced with "A moment of silence!" What does "moment of silence" even mean? Christmas is a federal holiday, but in government schools, it is a "bad word" and is instead called winter. Easter is now replaced with spring. But every non-Christian holiday is called by the actual name and often promoted and celebrated. Christians are effectively second or third-class citizens in the government schools. Students are literally ashamed to admit they are Christians.

Accommodations are made for every religion except Christians. During my nearly two decades at a particular school, Muslim students in our school were allowed out of class to pray as a school policy. If the Muslim students had a holiday, they got out of school as an excused absence. However, Christians are not given any accommodations for praying or worshipping during school. There are no excused holiday absences for Christians to take off.

Teachers in my school district all must either be Democrats or else keep their beliefs to themselves or face consequences. Democrats can hang posters of their favorite candidates, like Obama, including in the principal's office. It is all right if Democrat supporters wear buttons with their favorite candidate on their shirts. But if you were found with a button or poster for the Republican candidate, you were called to the office and warned not to endorse candidates.

The bias does not stop with Christians, males, non-Democrats, or white people. Heterosexual students or teachers must toe the line when speaking about marriage or sexuality. One meeting, teachers were told the district was going to be (and it held true) strictly enforcing any teacher or student using the word "gay" in any way even if the student is just joking around using the word. The gay students figured this new emphasis on their "rights" and took advantage immediately. Apparently the gay superintendent was on a mission to rid out dissention. The district offices, district websites, and district social media sites were all largely used to promote "pride" and "pride parades." Countless students and teachers had been disciplined for the most trivial and inadvertent use of the term or the topics associated with the word.

It is no wonder when parents find out about vouchers, many jump at the chance to escape the madness and marginalization their kids endure daily.

Chapter 8
"Walter's World" Students

While it is true that most students in Uncle Sam's plantation pass the standardized tests to graduate eventually, because of the emphasis on passing the tests, there are a lot of unintended consequences. Let's examine some of them.

If you ever watch Sean Hannity's "Man on the Street" or "Walter's World," it is not long before you can see how woefully ignorant many Americans are. If you don't know what "Walter's World" or "Man on the Street" are, just think of basic American history or political questions being asked to randomly chosen people on the street. Very few answer questions correctly, and most expose just how uninformed many Americans are about the world around them. I can vouch for the fact that most of the students that I have come across have been just as ignorant, not to be confused with incapable of learning. It is safe to say this is an American epidemic.

A recent poll from the University of Pennsylvania's Annenberg Public Policy Center revealed how shockingly little people know about even the most basic elements of our government and the Constitution that formed it. More than one in three people (37 percent) could not name a single right protected by the First Amendment. Only one in four (26 percent) can name all three branches of the government. In 2011, 38 percent could name all three branches. One in three (33 percent) can't name *any* branch of government.

How many times have we seen "Man on the Street" or "Walter's World" where individuals are questioned about basics in history or math and fail miserably? Why is this the case with all the standardized testing?

One study showed students were spending up to 110 hours for testing or preparing for testing. Not only is the time spent on testing taking away up to forty minutes per day of instruction time, but resources could be better spent. Testing costs upward of $1000 per student, money that could have went toward any number of instructional tools (Strauss).

What do the students learn in the plantation? The knowledge that they will be passed no matter how late they come or how often they miss class. Students understand doing homework is not necessary to pass since most teachers stop assigning homework to avoid high failure rates. Students are taught from the progressive-left perspective and discouraged from thinking outside of this box.

One time I gave students a survey based on platform issues of particular candidates. The parents took the survey. The score of the survey was tallied in front of the parents. When the parents found out the candidate they most agreed with was a Republican, parents became irate, and their children let me hear about the words shouted at them that the results were unquestionably wrong. On the other hand, if the choice was a Democrat, there was no feedback. Of course the majority of students knew not to step out of their box at home or at school unless they could handle the overwhelming brushback.

Colin Dunn explains in the book *Indoctrination*:

When kids started doing poorly on writing tests, elitists devised a new way to grade these exams, a way that ignores the rules of grammar in favor of the total impression of quality—whatever that's supposed to mean. Writing skills haven't improved, but students now feel better about their writing. (Source: indoctrination page 74)

Dunn leaves from the very first day of schooling, everything about schooling goes against Christian values. From discipline, philosophical points of view, the government schools are indoctrinating students in a way that is literally anti-biblical. But time doesn't leave it at that. The public school veteran teacher, police, and students are overdiagnosed and overmedicated while unlearning the truth of history and learning revisionist history instead.

The *Huffington Post* interviewed a teacher that explained the current education situation:

Apart from a few teachers who do train their students in critical thinking, most teachers do not for one simple reason— there is no time. State education departments mandate that so much material has to be covered that critical thinking cannot be taught, nor can the courses themselves be critically presented. In order to cover the curriculum, courses must be taught quickly, superficially, and uncritically, the infallible way of boring students. (Breslin, Huffington Post)

Most teachers either have their kids in private schools or wish they could. At a minimum, their kids are in affluent suburban schools. As one teacher put it, "I chose to teach in a public high school precisely because I pitied the children who felt forced to be at school, who felt trapped like I did when I was their age." The teacher contrasts her critique of the public schools with her child's promotion of the private school adding, "The kids take pride in their personal character, and they admit that they love learning."

This teacher had a lot more to say:

As I am writing this, I am observing a different class—one at the 825-student public high school where I teach. The educator's passion is evident, and his typed lesson plans are immaculate and thoughtful. It's not completely clear how fluent he is in the subject matter, however, because he has been interrupted or distracted by twenty things in twenty minutes: a pencil being sharpened, a paper bag being crumpled and tossed, a few irrelevant jokes that ignite several side conversations, a tardy student sauntering in with a smirk, a student feeding yogurt to a friend, a random class clown outside the window, and the subsequent need to lower the blinds, to name a few. The teacher is probably distracted by a disconcerting suspicion that he's talking primarily to himself. For the past half hour, I've been thinking about how I would teach this class—not what I would teach this class. (Godsey, *The Atlantic*)

This teacher speaks for most, if not just about all plantation teachers. This same teacher knows the danger in speaking out, I assume, which is why he stays anonymous. He goes on to explain that, "Unfortunately, the critical mass of engaged students and parents that's integral to creating this environment seems to be lacking at many of today's public schools. And it may be impossible to attain when everything is both free and compulsory."

There is no question schools in America are in bad academic shape. In many cases, it goes a lot further than just academics. Students and parents need to find what is in their best interests to minimize the "Walter's World" students.

Chapter 9
Diminished Morality in Schools

Eden Collinsworth: After spending a year exploring this topic, I think that we're not necessarily born with ethics or morality. I think that a great deal of it is acquired. (http://knowledge.wharton.upenn.edu/ article/decline-of-morality/)

Our Constitution was made only for a moral and religious people. It is wholly inadequate to the government of any other.

—John Adams

The negative consequences of losing much of our Christian foundation throughout the country and in particular affecting the children in Uncle Sam's plantation is very unfortunate. Frank Turek believes, "Secularizing public education has been the key to our nation's moral demise. Once public education went secular, the rest of society eventually did, especially when the products of that system became our leaders" (Turek, *Cross Examined*).

As Abraham Lincoln once explained, "The philosophy of the schoolroom in one generation will be the philosophy of the government in the next."

One of the arguments against school vouchers is that they somehow negatively impact our democracy. I agree with Frank Turek that the current situation without vouchers is creating immoral outcomes, and John Adams expressed these outcomes make our democracy inadequate. In other words, immoral people will destroy our country if we allow the immorally run Uncle Sam plantation schools to keep its near monopoly.

California, one of the nation's trendsetters, teaches inappropriate subjects and has extremely controversial perspective being taught as fact. Todd Starnes points out, "One of the nation's largest public school systems is preparing to include gender identity to its classroom curriculum, including lessons on sexual fluidity and spectrum— the idea that there's no such thing as one hundred percent boys or one hundred percent girls" (Starnes, "Gender Identity").

If the average parent could observe what goes on in the larger, especially inner city urban districts, the parent would quickly become an education-voucher supporter. Students freely use foul language in front of adults, wear clothing that shows too much cleavage for ladies, and sagging pants for guys, and much more.

What you see in the halls transitioning to class is bad enough, but inside and outside the classrooms leave much to be desired. In class, students openly talk about sex, drugs, and regularly about who will fight at lunch or after school. Students pass around a student's paper to copy off of and do not bother to hide their cheating.

One teacher, a serious Christian, said to me, "Can you just sense evil in this school?"

At the school I taught at for nearly two decades, I noticed the required reading or chosen reading lessons in class were authored by far-left progressives. I used to go in the hall and listen to teachers over and over say, "The white man did this to our people" or "did that to our people." And the more they spoke like that, the more likely they were to get advanced fast-tracked into much better pay within the district and put into leadership positions.

Science classes would teach evolution as if it were a fact and use the (easily debunked) Al Gore version of science as if it were fact. Kids thinking outside of this box were quickly put back in their place, and so were teachers. Science never mentions any theories to counter Darwin's theory; instead, the book of Genesis was taught in the Greek mythology unit. Meanwhile, seniors were given books that taught that all religions were really the same.

English teacher Paul Barnwell has come to this conclusion:

> A reluctance to teach about religions and value systems is coinciding with a steady decline of teen involvement in formal religious activity over the past 50 years, according to research led by San Diego State Professor Jean Twenge. And while attending church is only one way young people may begin to establish a moral identity, schools don't seem to be picking up the slack. There's undoubtedly a fear about what specific ethical beliefs and character traits schools might teach, but one answer might be to expose students

to tough issues in the context of academic work—not imposing values, but simply exploring them. (Barnwell, *The Atlantic*)

When Uncle Sam's schools do decide to work on values, there is swift pushback. Many will argue that these programs are politically motivated, often teaching children traditional and often conservative values. Naysayers say these programs are designed to create robotic students who do not question authority and will grow not questioning authority. Of course, proponents would say government schools are already producing robots and traditional values are shared values of society, not politically affiliated.

Archibald Alexander (A. A.) Hodge was an American Presbyterian leader and was the principal of Princeton Seminary between 1878 and 1886. Hodge believed:

I am as sure as I am of Christ's reign that a comprehensive and centralized system of national education, separated from religion, as is now commonly proposed, will prove the most appalling enginery for the propagation of anti-Christian and atheistic unbelief, and of anti-social nihilistic ethics, individual, social and political, which this sin-rent world has ever seen.[2]

Jesus made it quite clear when he said, "Whoever is not with me is against me, and whoever does not gather with me scatters." (Matt. 12:30, ESV). I am amazed at how many Christians refuse to acknowledge this fact as it relates to the government school system. Our education is either based on biblical truth or some other "alleged truth." There is no such thing as neutrality in this regard. All education is religious in nature. Since it is illegal for students in our government schools to be taught from a Christian perspective, then it follows that they must be taught from a non- (or anti) Christian perspective.

As Hodge pointed out, the result of non-Christian education is anti-Christian education. Government schools must be anti-Christian. They can be nothing else. Therefore, to send a child to a government school is to have them trained in an anti-Christian environment for fourteen thousand instructional hours. To get that much instruction from church, a child would have to attend two hours a week for 140 years!

---

2. http://teachdiligently.com/articles/aa-hodge-public-schools-are-the-engine-of-atheism

If you read article after article from the secular point of view, it implies the same thing—that public schools cannot be moral because morality is a relative word.

David Black, professor of New Testament and Greek, and Dr. M. O. Owens Jr., chair of New Testament studies at Southeastern Baptist Theological Seminary in Wake Forest, North Carolina, conclude:

> No academic skepticism, no secularist authors, no blatant materialism can so undermine the spiritual life of the country like the completely secularized training of the child under the authority of the state. Despite what Mr. (president) Bush says, Bible-based education is mandatory for Christian parents. If we think we can keep our children in a secular school system and escape the dumbed-down, amoral, and immoral results of secular humanism in schools, we are sorely mistaken. (Baucham, Exodusmandate.org)

The fact that I have taught the secular humanist at government schools myself, I can attest to David Black's statement being accurate. The vast majority of us who have experienced the difference between the government schools and Christian schools would argue that the state of the country will be in much better shape if more kids could escape to the Christian schools rather than remain trapped in the anti-Christian government schools.

Chapter 10
Flawed Arguments against Escaping the Plantation

The presence of education-choice options doesn't "destroy" public education, but it does make existing government schools step up their game, as Sarah A. Cordes wrote in a recent EdNext study titled "Charters and the Common Good"

The education-choice voucher naysayers often use a set of standard arguments to why parents should be not be allowed to leave Uncle Sam's plantation.

Let us explore the data-driven people.

While it might be true that in a snapshot of data, the public school that teaches to the test might in the near term perform better than the newly transitioning student coming from the public school, even in these cases the data is far from conclusive.

In Washington, D.C., the research shows little change in math and reading scores, but graduation rates and scholarship rates rose significantly. Parents also felt their children were in a much safer environment (US Dept. of Ed., 2010). There are tons of studies in America and in the US that are very recent follow-up studies that are very conclusive that education-choice vouchers are making enormous contributions. But to be honest, that is not the point.

Since when, in America, does government, backed by teacher unions, get to tell parents what is best for their children? Data can be used for and against the case for vouchers. But keeping parents from being able to choose how their money will be used for their own children is un-American. Parents should not be forced to keep their kids in an environment that teaches values in conflict with their own values. What are opponents afraid of?

Betsy Devos, the new secretary of education, gets many hyperbolic headlines like, "Devos is trying to advance God's Kingdom," or "Devos is coming for your public schools." Although the headlines are extreme and I am sure not Devos's intentions, the only way these headlines could come true are if parents are given the right and take this right to escape the public school system. Giving people a choice does not force them to leave the school system. But the presumption is very telling since the headlines in not-so-subtle ways indicate the parent would opt out of the plantation school system if given the choice.

My neighbor, who I am certain is much like many opponents of vouchers, made a disturbing admission. I asked him if he supported vouchers, and he said no. He claimed he supported public school education. I then asked, "So, did your children attend public schools?" One would assume the answer to be yes since he said he supported public schools. But apparently, he supported the public schools keeping the public school kids away from his children! I have a feeling that is the fear of many, that the public school students on vouchers might lead to the watering down of their children's quality and superior education.

In the book *Separating School and State* by Sheldon Richman, the case is made to stop all tax funding for and government involvement participation in educating school children. Richman argues, "People can and have the right to run their own lives." Richman makes a lot of great points in the book, but realistically, I do not see state funding of schools going away. Too many hands are already in the pot. One point by Richman I absolutely agree with is when government gets involved, it has strings attached, even with vouchers. Regulations overburden schools and lead to politicians making decisions about education that they are not qualified to make instead of the professionals on the ground floor.

Danny Weil, in his book *School Vouchers and Privatization,* lays out the data and arguments for and against redirecting money for school choice. Some argue the redistributing of the money hurts the public schools. I would argue that the public schools need to feel the financial pain to be able to redirect their energies and focus or fail to exist as a school. Giving failing schools more money is not a solution. After renovating the school I taught at, it cost taxpayers over forty million dollars, the scores got worse, not better.

Jady Green, in *Why America Needs School Choice,* concludes, "Happily, there are nine random assignment studies of participant effects that present ten analyses of voucher experiments. All of them have been peer-reviewed and published-all but one show significant positive results." Green went on to say that the National Education Association wrongly states voucher do not improve student achievement based on flawed research. In fact, even charter schools overall benefit students. And of course, if you add in private schools, Green says the evidence is clear do better academically.

Another big reason for the fear of vouchers is Christianity. A significant number of headlines about Devos pointing to her Christian views as an argument against her plans. At my former school district, the book of Genesis from the Bible was taught. But in what context was it taught? In the Greek mythology unit! There is a war against Christianity in public schools. It is not neutral.

Follow the money if you want to find the single largest factor in keeping parents from the choice of better schools for their children. It is no secret that the party that claims to be very supportive of choice is totally against school choice for parents. One of, if not their largest contributors are the teachers' unions. Public school teachers make far superior salary and benefits than their private and Christian school colleagues. It is no wonder the fear many have. But are the union interests in the best interests of the children? No.[3]

Christopher Emdin suggests to teachers in his book *For White Folks Who Teach in the Hood*: "Identifying the pedagogical processes that are rooted in the neoindigenous community."

In her book *Reign of Error*, Diane Ravitch concludes any efforts to reform schools that has to do with incentive-based instruction fails. Ravitch contends about teachers earning merit pay: "Most of their efforts were concen-

---

[3.] https://www.opensecrets.org/industries/indus.php?ind=L1300

trated on the students in the middle, who would show the biggest improvement."

In another Ravitch book *The Death and Life of the Great American School System*, privatization is the enemy of schools.

David Osborne in *Reinventing America's Schools*, believes public schools need to be saved, insisting, "By creating one of the world's first mass education systems, free to all children, we forged the most educated workforce in the world-a key pillar of our economic strength." While I won't try to argue against his point, I don't agree with the assessment that plantation schools need to be saved. The attempt to save public education by status quo solutions has been going on far too long.

A point Mr. Osborne and I can strongly agree on is we both believe that schools should have more flexibility and freedom to specialize on whichever style they fit, and parents and students could choose the best fit. Osborne likes the charter school model but not charter schools themselves. But Mr. Osborn and I part ways with his belief that schools will be improved by competing for dollars based on attendance. Just ask the countless school districts that have made headlines for fudging attendance and grades in order to get federal dollars.

David Osborne is a senior fellow at Progressive Institute, with the keyword being progressive. They are definitely a Democrat Party think tank that, I admit, have a lot of great points. Let's talk about a few of David Osborne's suggestions for the plantation system.

Osborne points to seven key strategies to transform urban school systems: creating clarity, contestability, school choice, decentralizing control, using freedom to transform the school culture, and boosting the capacity of school leaders, teachers, and other staff. None of these seem to be from the typical progressive mind-set. You have to dig deeper in the book to find the tragic flaws.

The fear of plantation schools gradually being overtaken by private schools because of the education vouchers seems to only be a fear if you have an unhealthy relationship with the political party that sustains and is sustained by the plantation system. If Osborne's intention is to make schools better, that competition makes schools improve, it shouldn't matter whether it's private or public. If Osborne really believes schools need to be more like charter schools, why is he so against leaving the plantation? Osborne makes a few more points that I really agree with but need to be tweaked a bit.

Schools, especially plantation schools included, will fudge the numbers to get their results. They hire data specialists to "clean up the data." A quick Google search will demonstrate how widespread fudging the numbers is.

Chapter 11
Uncle Sam's Plantation System Monopoly Needs to End

Andrew J. Coulson: The massive productivity advantage of private-sector education is not unique to Washington, D.C. (https://www.cato.org/publications/commentary/time-end-monopoly-education)

The system that forces public school children to stay in the schools that are contrary to the values taught at home is immoral. Currently, fifteen states have voucher programs. I not only believe the voucher programs are necessary, but I believe they need to be expanded.

What is a solution to dealing with Uncle Sam's plantation? Competition.

"Part of the appeal of school choice is that it allows families to find schools that work best given their particular situation" (Jay Green, *Why America Needs School Choice*).

I do not believe it took the countless research from Jay Green to make what one would think is a common-sense statement.

Some, like the National Education Association, claim a pure voucher system would only encourage economic, racial, and ethnic and religious stratification in our society. But Green counters, "Private school vouchers can further lesson residual income segregation and the segregation results are robust to alternative assumptions about school competition" (Greene).

One of the biggest arguments against escaping the plantation is that school choice undermines civic values. But after fifty-nine analyses of twenty-one studies done by Patrick Wolf of the University of Arkansas, in fifty-six analyses, choice schools did as well or better than traditional public schools at producing desired for civic values (Greene).

Athletes are not the only people that have to constantly improve in order to compete at the highest level. Currently the public schools don't have to compete very much at all. In the real world, if you don't compete, you go out of business, but for Uncle Sam's plantation, the worse you do the more money you get!

I happened to teach at one of the worst-performing schools in the state. If you want to see a poorly operated school, just keep throwing money at it every time the school gets low scores on standardized tests. In our case, they even brought us the most expensive school at one point in the state, spending over forty-two million dollars to renovate the building. Did scores improve? No!

Star Parker has a chapter in her revised edition book entitled *Uncle Sam's Plantation* dedicated to education in government schools called Uncle Sam's Education, which mentions how the Obama administration pulled the plug on a successful and popular voucher program. Parker tells, "The vouchers valued up to $7,500 per scholarship, cost less than half of the $17,000 per student that D.C. spends to maintain one of the worst public school systems in the country."

In Ohio, the EdChoice Voucher payout is currently $4,650 for grades K-8 and $6,000 for grades 9- 12. EdChoice will pay either the scholarship amount or the private school's actual tuition amount, whichever is less. However, the state average per student expense is $11,637. I believe voucher students are being shortchanged. Why does the public school get the entire amount, but the

Christian or private school only gets a small fraction of the entire amount?

If your child is in a public school and the school is meeting your child's needs and is acceptable to you as a parent, you can stay put. Parents with kids attending a school or school system, which is promoting values that are contrary to those you want your child to bring home, should have the option of opting out of this school or school system.

I have watched countless ambitious students over the years being dragged into some of the worst habits that they carried into adulthood. Several of my students were killed just down the road from the school because of school incidents and gangs within the school. Several of my students have been put in jail for killing students in the school. Why would kids be forced to attend this school?

If the public were informed of just the conversations in the hall or in the classroom that are allowed and are in routine, the call for vouchers surely would escalate.

Why You Should Escape the Compulsory Plantation

Einstein's quote about public school: "The coercion had such a deterring effect that after I pass the final examination I found the consideration of any scientific problems distasteful for me for an entire year" (Separating School and State).

Speaking from experience, my wife was actually a delegate to an NEA meeting that was more of a socialist propaganda experience than anything else. The NEA uses language directly coming from the United Nations and the Communist Manifesto.

What's the big deal about this?

Vladimir Lenin once said, "Give me four years to teach children in the seat I have sown will never be uprooted."

Socialist Party of American candidate Norman Thomas, after running for president from 1928–1948, said he was retiring because both the Democratic and Republican parties had adopted every plank of the socialist platform, and there was no longer a need for the alternative Socialist Party. Incremental progressivism, supported by Uncle Sam's plantation, allows for the dissolving of our individualistic society. As Jim Marrs alludes to, as socialism becomes pervasive, so does the loss of individuality. (Jim Marrs, *The Trillion-Dollar Conspiracy*, 11–13)

Influenced by the socialist model, teacher contracts are almost always in favor of experience over quality and with the expectation of benefits not based on results. Of course, this is un-American in an unproductive way of getting the best results.

"He alone, who owns the youth, gains the future" (Adolf Hitler)[4]. There definitely plenty of reasons to Uncle Sam's plantation, and many reasons they don't want you to escape.

Communism, from its inception to current history, seeks to eliminate Christians or any other religion for that matter. To this day, churches are being harassed or taken down in China. The same used to be true in Russia, in the Soviet Union. Socialism is just communism-lite. Uncle Sam's plantation marginalizes Christians and hostile toward Christians.

Not only is the plantation forcing its regressive ideology on students, but the federal bureaucracy creates a problem with its rules for special education students.

The ten-day suspension maximum rule days out of school for special education damages the school climate. These students realize the administrators are trying to "save" the 10 days for a serious offense. So often times these students do just enough disrupting so no to trigger

[4.] Adolf Hitler Quotes. (n.d.). BrainyQuote.com. Retrieved February 5, 2018, from BrainyQuote.com Web site: https://www.brainyquote.com/quotes/adolf_hitler_378177

the suspension. Ultimately this really hurts the school climate immensely

Discipline incidents are increasing but are not being dealt with. Schools are too worried about being called racists or are maybe just trying to demonstrate (doctored) improvement, and so for whatever the motivation is, discipline reports are not even close to being accurate. Teachers in my district, the largest in Ohio, were regularly reporting to the union to get arbitration to deal with the discipline reports, called 190s, not being processed by administrators. The 190s are supposed to be acted on within seventy-two hours. A carbon copy of the action taken is supposed to be sent back to the teacher.

Students often would come back to the teacher that just sent the student down to the office with a 190 and brag that the administrator tore up the 190. Not only was the 190 not dealt with, but the child won a victory by coming back to class unscathed. What a joke!

Consequently, teachers find ways to take matters into their own hands, handling discipline by alternative methods to avoid the coddling administration. To be fair, there is pressure from above the administration that sadly encourages and incentivizes the low number of 190s documented. Each 190 is supposed to be electronically filed.

John Taylor Gatto, former New York State and New York City Teacher of the Year and the author of *The Underground History of America,* argues, "Mandatory education serves children only incidentally; its real purpose is to turn them into servants." Based on my two decades long history of instruction, I don't disagree. Very few students do more than beat the system choose to achieve what is expected of them by their parent or major influences. Each year, I have taught only a handful of students who were passionate about learning.

Glenn Beck explains,

> I could go on and on. My point is this: the folks that adopted this set of goals in the 60s (Hillary, BHO, Alinsky, Ayres, Van Jones etc, etc, etc are simply executing on the plan. They are taking the long term view and have converted the democrat party into the vehicle to get them across the finish line. The democrat platform is indistinguishable from the communist platform. (Beck, *Conform*)

Beck's view is accurate when it comes to the goals of government schools. The Democrat platform and government schools backed by unions that exclusively support Democratic candidates and their agendas. Government schools are largely propaganda machines in primary and secondary schools. Any hint to stepping outside the agenda box, like mentioning the word God or positively recognizing a Republican candidate, is swiftly dealt with.

One way to keep the massive government machine working is by incentivizing dependency on various programs. Overdiagnosis of ADHD just being done by schools and doctors. So what is your day of the students are just hyper, and schools have trouble controlling them in the one-size-fits-all plantation (Marrs, *The Trillion-Dollar Conspiracy*).

From my own experience, medicine would often take a hyper kid (usually a boy) and turn them into a zombie. Boys often need to be able to move around to make learning for them easier. This might take creativity by the teacher to avoid a medical solution.

Chapter 12
The Escape

Choice in education is not when a student picks a different classroom in this building or that building, uses this voucher or that tax-credit scholarship. Choice in education is bigger than that. Those are just mechanisms," she said. "It's about freedom to learn. Freedom to learn differently. Freedom to explore. Freedom to fail, to learn from falling and to get back up and try again. It's freedom to find the best way to learn and grow ... to find the exciting and engaging combination that unlocks individual potential.

—Betsy Devos[5]

If you want to stay at Uncle Sam's plantation, you have the right to do that. If you want to shelter your kid by

---

5. http://www.wpxi.com/news/trending-now/betsy-devos-common-core-is-dead-at-us-department-of-education/685118228) 1/23/18

homeschooling them or using an online school, that is also acceptable. If your best option is a Christian education, then for sure you should have your children have this for an option. Whether you want the fancy restaurant or the smorgasbord buffet, the right to choose is the most logical and free decision in what used to be considered the freest country in the world.

Education vouchers, as they are currently used in American, are a great start but fall very short of being given the status and funding on par with the Uncle Sam's plantation system.

A Case for Vouchers[6]

Scott Walker reduced the power of unions in Wisconsin, and a Colorado law allowed the Douglas County board in Colorado to reduce the union power. In both cases, this reduction in the union stranglehold allowed for positive reforms to take place that significantly improved academics.

[6.] https://www.pbs.org/wgbh/pages/frontline/shows/vouchers/choice/provouchers.html

Reasons … Benefits[7]

One reason current education-choice vouchers fall short is the stipulations attached with the vouchers. These stipulations take away from school autonomy. A big part of school problems in the plantation schools are the government restraints and mandates!

Parents that want to keep their kids in schools with government restraints ought to be allowed to in the government schools. There are public schools, particularly in the suburbs, that have high graduation rates as well as high test scores when compared locally or even nationally. And often, they have many successful extracurricular activities, sports, and sports that are above and beyond what the norm is. It is understandable why parents would want to keep their children in a successful school.

On the other hand, parents who want their children to go to schools that are not overregulated by the government should also have that choice. Politicians nor unions should have control over where or how students are educated; that decision should be for the parents.

If a parent wants to homeschool their child, it should not be for the government to discourage this or even reg-

---

[7.] http://www.businessinsider.com/why-kids-should-get-homeschooled-2016-8

ulate homeschooling. Or maybe the parent wants to send their children to an alternative school that may not have certified teachers, but the instructors are professionals with practical expertise.

There are former authors of books that might want to teach English but are not certified by the state to teach English, or former engineers that might want to teach math or physics that are not certified by the state. But who would say an engineer or an author would not be qualified to teach subjects they use daily from their profession? Teachers' unions might say that or maybe politicians funded by these unions, but many parents might find this alternate education model more conducive for their children.

Today, 250 kids at the school that I currently teach at got to witness testimonies that gave the glory to God. Eighty percent of the students that were blessed with this experience were there because of education vouchers. Fortunately, my boys who attend the school also were very blessed with this great experience as well. Unfortunately, if the 80 percent of the students were not blessed with education vouchers, this life-changing experience would not have been witnessed by them. The testimonies that were very personal and hard to express would not have had the same forum in a public school.

Students don't have to grow up as fast in a Christian school. For example: middle school kids say they are dating even though the most they do is talk to each other in class or text each other on the phone. Middle school kids in most public schools are far more expressive on average.[8]

Maybe you don't believe your kid should be exposed to gender confusion. How many parents believe there's just male and female and believe transgenderism is not a gender but possibly gender confusion? One Bentley middle school believed it was appropriate to have the students choose which identity they identify with by asking them to choose:

a) Male

b) Female

c) Transgender (M to F)

d) Transgender (F to M)

What about when Obama used executive order to enforce his transgender bathroom policy? Obama had instructed public schools last May to let transgender students use the bathrooms matching their chosen gender identity, threatening to withhold funding for schools that did not comply.[9]

---

8. http://www.foxnews.com/story/2007/10/18/middle-school-gives-students-birth-control-pill.html

9. https://www.reuters.com/article/us-usa-trump-lgbt/trump-revokes-obama-guidelines-on-transgender-bathrooms-idUSKBN161243 2-6-18

Maybe some parents didn't want their daughter to have to use the same restroom with a boy.[10]

Who knows what the absurd plan the next president after Trump will blackmail plantation schools into doing next?

Speaking about the amendment (led by far-leftist senator in my state of Ohio Sherrod Brown) to the Every Student Achieves Act: "This is modeled after the soviet system," said Charlotte Iserbyt, author of *Deliberate Dumbing Down of America* and a former senior policy advisor at the US Department of Education. "It is part of a long-range plan outlined by the Carnegie Corporation to abolish local elected boards and use education to transform America from a capitalist system to a planned economy."

Whether it's the federal government, the state government, or even the local government, any government control is part of Uncle Sam's plantation. Slavery has always been morally wrong and is an inefficient way of life. It's good to know that most will probably choose to leave the plantation, which is why the plantation does not want to give its constituents the choice.

[10.] http://www.thegeorgetowndish.com/thedish/
parents-upset-sex-test-hardy-middle-school

A recent poll conducted shows the support of education vouchers:

> Minority Americans also tend to support school choice, including 72 percent of Latinos and 66 percent of African Americans. About six in ten white Americans support school choice. Meanwhile, majorities of every political group support school choice: 75 percent of Republicans, 62 percent of independents, and 54 percent of Democrats, along with 64 percent of Millennials.[11]

As you can see, education choice is very popular among all groups except Democrats. To that, I say the Democrats can keep their children in the plantation schools if they would like. But let the other parents choose the school that best fits their children.[12]

One public school district in Minnesota is teaching radical social justice to five-year-olds. I'm not sure if the children

---

[11.] https://www.nationalreview.com/corner/
school-choice-poll-two-thirds-americans-support-education-reform/

[12.] http://amp.nationalreview.com/corner/455529/school-choice-poll-two-thirds-americans-support-it (2-6-18)

that have families on welfare feel privileged or understand what it means to be privileged. However, that won't stop the plantation system from indoctrinating the concept.[13]

One *New York Times* article, which I believe is almost as laughable as it could be, believes parents are too stupid to make good decisions on where their child should go to school. David Leonhardt, when explaining why education-choice vouchers (in his opinion) fail, said, "For the most part, though, identifying a good school is hard for parents." He goes on to say charters should be a better option than vouchers. Which I think is quite laughable since for the past twenty years, I've been hearing how unsuccessful charter schools are by the same people. I think what is really going on is they realize the momentum of education-choice vouchers, and they are trying to put in a stopgap measure.[14]

Jeremy Kelly writes, "The point of Ohio's primary EdChoice voucher program has been to give students from under-performing public schools the opportunity to attend participating private schools, according to the Ohio Department of Education." In other words, the parents

---

13. https://www.westernjournal.com/public-schools-now-forcing-kindergarten-students-study-white-privilege/?utm_source=facebook&utm_medium=thenewvoice&utm_campaign=can&utm_content=2018-02-04

14. https://mobile.nytimes.com/2017/05/02/opinion/school-vouchers-charters-betsy-evos.html?referer=https://www.google.com/ 2-6-18

will have an opportunity to choose what is in their child's best interest.[15]

If given the choice, would you want a choice?[16]

> Not until I went into the churches of America and heard her pulpits flame with righteousness did I understand the secret of her genius and power. America is great because America is good, and if America ever ceases to be good, America will cease to be great.[17]

"It is the little details that are vital. Little things make big things happen" (John Wooden).

Getting into a debate about education-choice vouchers, the anti-school choice side argues public school students in some studies fair better in the public schools. There is also the argument that public schools are necessary for students to be connected to their community and not just motivated by financial potential. Of course, these arguments can be dismantled and miss the biggest point.

15. http://www.mydaytondailynews.com/news/ohio-school-vouchers-expand-kettering-lawmaker-opposes-program/yrVmmhnHP4jjkmNrQj61wO/, 2-7-18
16. https://www.goodreads.com/author/quotes/465.Alexis_de_Tocqueville
17. http://www.azquotes.com/author/14691-Alexis_de_Tocqueville 1/19/2018

Protestant Christian schools are already among the top 10 percent of schools when judged by average student performance on the NAEP test. For the past thirty-seven years, since ACSI and its predecessors started tracking Stanford Achievement Test scores in 1974, ACSI schools have scored significantly higher than the national norm in every grade level every year. Clearly Protestant Christian schools, and ACSI schools specifically, are excelling academically.[18]

Clearly, based on nearly four decades of evidence, Christian schools are an academic alternative to Uncle Sam's plantation. When students transfer from failing public schools, as some studies initially cite, the students might have to adjust to the new climate, rigor, and the realization they often will need to get caught up.

The same study debunks that the private school kids lose their sense of community. As a matter of fact, students in the Christian schools tend to be active in their commu-

---

[18.] https://alchristian.com/2013/02/the-christian-school-difference/
https://www.acsi.org/resources/csc/christian-school-comment-archive/445-the-christian-school-difference

nity church, earn less, but give more back to the community. If students attend ACSI-accredited schools, the numbers go even further.[19]

Academics in accredited ACSI Christian schools are on average better than non-accredited schools. However, the 69 percent of administrators in these accredited schools said their top priorities for students were development of Christian worldview, involvement in evangelism, or a close personal relationship with God. Meanwhile, 80 percent of public school principals said their top priority was for student basic literacy.[20] School-choice vouchers are not just about academic freedom but spiritual priorities. Some parents want their kids to develop a closer relationship with their creator.

Personally, I love teaching in a Christian school even though my salary is less than half as much as what I was bringing home previously in the plantation school system. Teaching in a Christian school is freedom at last! Jesus is no longer a bad word. I can pray for and with students. The school climate is so positive, and the parents are far more supportive of the teachers. Parents thank the teachers for

---

[19.] 44.5 the Christian School Difference by Dan Egeler, https://www.acsi.org/resources/csc/christian-school-comment-archive/445-the-christian-school-difference, 1-4-2018

[20.] http://www.biblecenterschool.com/wp-content/uploads/2016/02/ACSI-World-Class-Schools-Accredited.pdf, 1-4-2018

contacting them. The experience is 180 degrees different from the public school experience.

The halls at my new teaching assignment are filled with students who come from an overall similar socioeconomic status like in Uncle Sam's plantation, but here the atmosphere is pleasant and civil. The halls at my previous job in the public school is in sharp contrast, loud insults and foul language, and regular fighting were the norm for decades teaching there.

The race and ethnic backgrounds are strikingly similar, as are the colors in the halls and on the team jerseys, but the schools could not be farther apart. So why the difference in atmosphere?

Of course, there are many factors that contribute to why Christian schools can take the same students the inner-city schools cannot handle and have success. Christian school teachers get paid less than half of what big city public school teachers make but have much more success with the same students. I am not implying they are better teachers, but I am saying something must account for the better climate in the Christian schools.

What is different in Christian schools? From day one in science class in Uncle Sam's plantation, students learn Darwin's version of life, that their very existence is an accident, that they are no more important than the animals they dissect. Often, kids are struggling in foster care, living with abuse, etc. In the Christian school, there is Bible instruction, weekly chapel, and a school based on love, Jesus's teachings offer hope to the lost.

Not one time since teaching at the Christian school that I am currently teaching at has any teacher or administrator suggested or implied teaching to the standardized test. In the public schools, that is what the curriculum is centered around. At times, students just learn from former tests and get out of class to focus on passing whatever standardized test is forthcoming. It is no wonder that some government school students have done better with comparative newly-transferred students coming from public schools, still adjusting to the new atmosphere in the voucher school.

Even though my current school has had recent temporary setbacks with standardized math scores, this largely attributed to the last two math teachers having attendance problems due to illness. Instead of remedying the situation with focusing around the tests and on what the students scored low on, the new math teachers decided to get students working during school and for homework on a program designed to help improve in specific per student issues in math. The remedy allows for teachers to continue working on the math that students most need to know for the current course. In other words, the teachers do not spend their days teaching to the upcoming standardized test. In the government schools, the vast majority of the focus is teaching to the test.

The conversation in the Christian school is much more open; there's no need to be politically correct. There is a diversity of opinions, but the common thread is core biblical values. Morality issues can be answered through scripture while research does not have to exclude Christian scientists or expressing science perspective from a creator and purposeful designer perspective.

Not one time have I heard a conversation in during my Christian school employment that has been about the current president or previous. The past two decades in the Uncle Sam's plantation was caustic politically. Just telling the truth about Bill Clinton or Barack Obama could put a teacher in the hot seat. But supporters of the two presidents could regularly break the rules set by board of education as long as the candidate was a Democrat. Of course, the union almost exclusively supports every agenda and candidate the Democrats have in office or running for office.

Christian schools that currently accept education vouchers do have some hurdles because of the strings attached by Uncle Sam for accepting state funds. However, Christian schools are the best choice for education based on the fact that Christian schools can use their own school books of choice (including books that are Christian based), have chapel, read from the Bible, include God and other biblical truths into their lessons, and in general, do not fear the use and input from the Word of God. In other words, you get the best of both worlds, learning Bible-based truths and morality while getting a quality education.

Uncle Sam's Plantation School System

"The idea that *To Kill a Mockingbird*—a book that sought to expose racial injustice—is now considered racially offensive is beyond words," Todd Starnes points out. The new censorship in the plantation schools is feeling more Orwellian than ever.[21]

Star Parker says it best: "Liberating our kids from the cesspools in our urban areas that we call public schools is the great "civil rights challenge" of our time. (*Uncle Sam's Plantation*, 2010, 141) I would add to this statement that

---

[21.] https://www.toddstarnes.com/show/school-drops-beloved-literary-classics-oppressive-language/

suburban schools might have excellent academic standing, they too are in trouble and need to escape.

College and professional sports teams are realizing huge benefits attributing to Bible study and uniting in Christ.

I have been attending the annual Ohio State University Football Coaches Clinic for about seven years. Jim Tressel had a huge Christian influence on his team and encouraged his players to join Athletes in Action, a Christian program for athletes to be actively discipled and be disciples. Even after Tressel retired, the program is swelling with disciples, especially from the football team. Urban Meyer spoke at the clinic I attended and spoke of the Athletes in Action being instrumental in his team's success. Meyer said attendance is voluntary, but he said 99 percent of his team participates in the program!

The last four teams the Buckeyes had were led by a strong Christian man that was part of Athletes in Action, the hustle point guard Aaron Craft. I was blessed to hear him speak at a couple of functions about his personal relationship with Jesus Christ.

In 2013, NBA's Golden State Warriors were led by a coach who happened to double as a pastor. His team followed his Christian inspirational lead with daily Bible studies and pregame chapel. "The players will tell you the team's faith is part of the reason no Warrior has found his way into trouble with drunken-driving arrests or sexting scandals. You won't hear explicit rap songs blasting when you enter the locker room, and foul language is scarce. No one's noticeably disgruntled about contracts or playing time," says Marcus Thompson. Mark Jackson was fired but Golden State kept their Bible studies and chapel habits, attributing both to uniting a once fractured team, propelling it to two (so far) NBA titles since Jackson left.[22]

Faith is playing a primary role in the Philadelphia Eagles' lives, players, and coaches, including the head coach, Doug Pederson. There are weekly Bible studies at the facility, scripture text chains, and late-night prayer sessions at the team hotel the night before each game.

The Eagles were forced to overcome huge in 2018 playing against the legend Tom Brady, especially since starting quarterback Wentz went out injured in week fourteen that ended his MVP caliber season. Despite the adversity, the Eagles stayed strong together as a team largely because of their faith in Christ.[23]

---

22. https://www.mercurynews.com/2013/04/19/golden-state-warriors-lean-on-their-faith-heading-into-playoffs/, Feb 18, 2018
23. https://www.cnsnews.com/commentary/john-stonestreet/phillys-faith-filled-football-champs-story-behind-super-bowl-win, Feb 18, 2018

The values taught in scripture are truly ingrained in our culture but have been suppressed, attacked, and certainly not promoted in our culture. Values like humans are alive for a bigger purpose than just themselves, putting God first (not God's creation), humility, hard work, abstinence until marriage, be fruitful and multiply, and most importantly, that God planned each life for a purpose.

Ostensibly, Christian schools are teaching values that have helped create the most successful country in the history of mankind. We are a country that values equality and freedom.

Alex de Tocqueville said it best,

> Democracy extends the sphere of individual freedom, socialism restricts it. Democracy attaches all possible value to each man; socialism makes each man a mere agent, a mere number. Democracy and socialism have nothing in common but one word: equality. But notice the difference: while democracy seeks equality in liberty, socialism seeks equality in restraint and servitude.[24]

---

24. http://www.americanthinker.com/2014/09/the_stealing_of_the_american_state.html#ixzz57W9k361o, Feb 18, 2018

Religion, to de Tocqueville, should be considered the first of America's political institutions and even that is necessary for Americans to maintain Christianity at all cost. He correctly points out that America's unique view and value of equality before God and as citizens.[25]

De Tocqueville beautifully stated, "Liberty sees in religion the handmaiden of its struggles and triumphs, the cradle of its infancy, the divine source of its rights. She sees religion as the safeguard of morality, and morality as the guarantee of the laws and of its own posterity."[26]

"The American Republic will endure until the day Congress discovers that it can bribe the public with the public's money."[27]

As Russian sociologist Mikhail Tarusin puts it, "A non-believer is unpredictable, can do anything. A believer has in his soul a system of restraints. When the Russian people realize this, maybe there will be hope for change."

---

25. http://thefederalist.com/2013/11/21/two-things-tocqueville-says-matter-american-democracy-two-things-going-away/, Feb 18, 2018

26. https://www.heritage.org/civil-society/report/tocqueville-christianity-and-american-democracy, Feb 18, 2018

27. http://www.americanthinker.com/2014/09/the_stealing_of_the_american_state.html#ixzz57W95N3uR, Feb 18, 2018

I say America needs to stop heading down the path Russia is living in. We see some of the negative consequences already to the result of our degraded morals.[28]

The attacks on Christians are evident throughout the courts, and case law is attempting to usurp and redefine the once-revered US Constitution. Progressives rule the public schools from preschool to college. Judges seem to vote party line just like congress. Morality seems to take a backseat to party affiliation.

Many parents, like myself, might not like the direction of Uncle Sam's indoctrinating schools. One thing I know about students and oftentimes adults is that "One believes things because one has been conditioned to believe them," (Aldous Huxley, *Brave New World*). Public schools begin indoctrination of anti-Christian, progressive, anti-capitalist agenda.

If you want to have your kids going to schools that teach something came from nothing as leading atheist Richard Dawkins claims, you should have that right. But if you want your child to learn the biblical claims to creation, your child must escape the plantation schools.

[28.] https://www.heritage.org/report/corruption-russia-no-democracy-without-morality, Feb 18, 2018

Chapter 13
Conclusion

The calls for choice are becoming louder by the day. It is amazing that Uncle Sam's plantation schools have been able to operate their virtual monopoly for so long and face such little resistance.

I warned my high school friend to avoid putting his kids into the plantation system. My friend EJ and his wife have five children that are school age. He tried to keep them in Catholic schools, but he simply cannot afford to pay for all of them to attend. This past year, he lived to regret putting his quadruplets into a plantation school. EJ was regretfully confirming to me what I warned him about that came true.

EJ said he loved the teachers his children had, but what the kids were exposed to was unacceptable. His kids were only in the third grade but were coming home repeating or reenacting the immoral behavior and age inappropriate language and conversations. Simply put, EJ and his wife were shocked so much that they were willing to go broke to make the escape and expeditiously get their kids back into the Catholic schools, escaping the inferior education and social degradation the plantation the quadruplets had unfortunately endured for an entire calendar school year.

Although there is no such thing as a perfect school or school system, there is a school where opportunity is afforded to all parents and students to at least have the choice to find that school that is the best fit. The one size fits all model for schools has not worked and will never work. Schools might want to specialize in the arts, maybe another, the sciences, another might focus on trade professions, or even a Spanish-emersion school.

Michael Grable makes a great point, "The American Republic will endure until the day Congress discovers that it can bribe the public with the public's money" (Grable,

Stealing of the American State). Rush Limbaugh says something similar about congress being run by lobbyists. The current situation in schools is unfair to Christian school teachers who are paid half of what public school teachers make and to parents and students who suffer from being stuck in Uncle Sam's plantation schools.

It really shouldn't matter if unions or politicians think compulsory education is a necessary good and should be allowed to force students to attend government schools. What Americans deserve is the choice to find the best situation for their children. The arguments have been recycled for many years and the pro-government schools side has gotten their way for decades.

In 1989, the Wisconsin legislature was a trailblazer in passing a law allowing for education vouchers, targeting students from low-income households in the Milwaukee. Fast forward to 2011, Indian has a statewide voucher system.

"By 2017, Indiana's statewide voucher program is now the largest of its kind in the country and, with President Trump and Education Secretary Betsy DeVos openly encouraging states to embrace private school choice, the story of the Choice Scholarship—how it came to be, how it works and whom it serves—has become a national story of freedom, faith, poverty and politics," Corey Turner points out.[29]

Vouchers have expanded to 15 states.[30]

> An EdChoice survey of voucher parents, conducted last summer, is instructive. Among the top-five reasons parents cited for enrolling their child in a private school, "better academics" ranked second, not first. At the top of the list was "religious environment/instruction." (NPR, The Promise and Peril of School Vouchers)

I'm sure some would have a problem with the reasoning of someone using a voucher for religion being a priority in a parent's view of education. But one could argue it was the antipathy toward God in schools that made so many parents seek a religious school. Or maybe parents believe the Bible might have a say in the "truths" of necessary for life taught in schools.

[29.] https://www.npr.org/sections/ed/2017/05/12/520111511/
the-promise-and-peril-of-school-vouchers

[30.] https://www.edchoice.org/resource-hub/fast-facts/#voucher-fast-facts

States should Break Up these institutional schools decertify teaching let anyone who has a mind to teach bit for customers privatize this whole business trust the free market system ... We need less school not more. (Gatto)

Zachary Slayback said,

> My best teachers were those who do not
> follow the exam requirements and only
> begrudgingly made sure that the exam for
> completed ... the worst were those too
> obsessed with meeting state mandated
> standards. Most of your government
> schools have pay incentives for admin-
> istrators and features for increase results
> on standardized tests ... which means
> the government schools incentivized bad
> teaching. (Dumbing us Down)

One of the limitations of current voucher system in most states is the stranglehold of state rules and regulations attached with the funding. All the over burdensome rules in part is responsible for many of the problems we have in Uncle Sam's plantation system.

The money per child for government schools is far more than the current vouchers provide. One negative consequence of this is limiting the teacher pool to hire from. My school was pursuing a computer teacher to teach coding but lost the opportunity because he was lured away for twice as much pay at a government school. It's unfortunate for our students because this is too common.

Why aren't students allowed to have the money attached to them attending Uncle Sam's schools be allotted to the student to use for whichever school they would like to attend? Failing schools, like my previous employment, should not be getting more money to do less and be rewarded with more funding to try new programs to perpetually fail. Instead of constantly rewarding failure, let the students find better alternatives, which might include a private school.

Plantation schools are not incentivized to improve because of the lack of alternatives of the clientele. If government schools were forced to improve via pressure from competition, society would benefit. However, some schools, even with the increased competition, might fail to improve and therefore necessarily close or be downsized.

The main argument against school-choice vouchers is that the vouchers take money away from the government schools and therefore negatively impact the government schools. While this might be true, this does not mean the student is not still the beneficiary. Students do get an education to keep the plantation solvent, but schools exist to prepare students for life.

At the Christian school I am teaching at, there are teachers and leaders in the building that represent all different political spectrums. When kids are taught at any school, inevitably, the teacher's perspective influences the class. In the plantation schools, only one political perspective is tolerable, which limits students in their ability to realize there are a variety of passionate and comparable viewpoints.

Every day in America, we are inundated with data showing how poorly American schools are doing. Of course, government schools are overburdened with regulations and overcrowded classrooms that they are slow to fix their inherent problems.

Teacher unions help keep poor teachers from being removed from the classroom and discourage teachers from getting better at their jobs by getting contracts based on experience and not productivity. I witnessed for nearly two decades poor teachers with no classroom control getting paid the same as the best teachers in the building because pay is based on years of teaching experience, not how well you do your job. Effectively, unionized teachers have very little incentive, at least financial, to be great at what they do. There are great unionized teachers, but far too many poor teachers teach for decades and negatively impact students and schools while getting paid a handsome salary, twice as much as their private school competition.

When there is a scandal with the government schools, the consequence is minimal. But if a private school or a charter school has any improprieties, the consequence is severe and swift. The government schools are treated as though they are too big to fail.

My neighbor was telling me how he supported public schools but not education vouchers. I asked this neighbor where his kids went to school, and as I predicted, his sons were private school students. Most of the teachers I taught with in the government schools put their kids in private schools also.

I pay taxes for property, a separate school tax, local tax, federal taxes, etc. I do not find it fair to have to pay for my children twice to go to school.

About the Author

Edward Temple has been a certified math and social studies secondary school teacher since 1997. His experience in teaching includes low socioeconomic school districts that include Florida, Ohio, and Pennsylvania. Mr. Temple's teaching experience includes teaching public schools in both small rural and large inner-city schools. Currently, Mr. Temple is teaching at a Christian school that includes students from both the city and the rural areas. Besides teaching, Mr. Temple enjoys coaching and mentoring youth, and loves listening to sermons at church or on the radio. This author knew since the second grade he was going to be a teacher and has been teaching since 1997. He is a husband for nearly eighteen years and a father of twin boys that attend the school he teaches in. Mr. Temple is the youngest of six children that all attended the largest public school system in Ohio.

CPSIA information can be obtained
at www.ICGtesting.com
Printed in the USA
LVHW050750040319
609389LV00014B/351/P